DATE DUE			

Canoeing

BY M. J. YORK

The Child's World

Published by The Child's World®
1980 Lookout Drive • Mankato, MN 56003-1705
800-599-READ • www.childsworld.com

Acknowledgments
The Child's World®: Mary Berendes, Publishing Director
Red Line Editorial: Editorial direction
The Design Lab: Design
Amnet: Production

Photographs ©: Elena Elisseeva/Shutterstock Images, cover
(center), 1 (center), 20; Rob Marmion/Shutterstock Images,
back cover (bottom), 18; Shutterstock Images, cover (top),
cover (bottom), back cover (top), 1 (top), 1 (bottom), 12–13,
15, 16, 21; PhotoDisc, back cover (middle), 3, 11;
SportingImages, 4; Hemera/Thinkstock 6–7; AdStock RF/
Shutterstock Images, 8; iStock/Thinkstock, 9, 17; Stockbyte/
Thinkstock, 10; Comstock/Thinkstock, 14; Abel Tumik/
Shutterstock Images, 19

ISBN 9781626873285
LCCN 2014930662

Printed in the United States of America
Mankato, MN
July, 2014
PA02222

ABOUT THE AUTHOR

M. J. York is a children's author and editor who lives in Minnesota. She has loved the outdoors her entire life and started camping, hiking, and canoeing at a young age.

CONTENTS

OUT ON THE WATER

Have you ever seen mist rise off a lake at sunrise? Or, have you seen deer come down to the water to drink? Maybe you have gone

Enjoy nature from the seat of a canoe.

fishing and seen fish jump. Or maybe you've watched rushing **rapids**.

These are all things people may see when they go canoeing. They take a canoe out on the water. They **paddle** to get where they are going. Canoeing gives you a view of nature you cannot get from shore.

SEEING WILDLIFE

You can see a lot of **wildlife** from a canoe. Some animals live in water. Others come to drink or find food. You might see these animals in or around ponds, lakes, streams, or rivers:
- trout, catfish, bass, and sunfish
- turtles, frogs, and snakes
- dragonflies and butterflies
- ducks, geese, swans, herons, egrets, and eagles
- raccoons, beavers, muskrats, and deer

WHAT IS CANOEING?

A canoe is an open boat that comes to a point at its front and back ends. People sit

Face forward when you paddle a canoe.

facing forward. They use paddles to move along the water. Often, two people paddle together.

People around the world have used canoes for thousands of years. Today's canoes are similar to the ones Native Americans have

used for **centuries**. They stretched animal skins or birch bark over light, wooden frames. In the far north, people made canoe frames out of whalebone. Others shaped canoes out of tree trunks. Today, canoes are usually made from light metal or **fiberglass**. But the design has changed little from early canoes.

Early canoes were sometimes carved out of tree trunks.

TRAVELING BY CANOE

Native Americans used canoes for **transportation**. They fished and gathered food from lakes and streams. When Europeans came to North America, they started using canoes, too. French fur traders called voyageurs brought furs from the deep woods out to trading posts. They paddled 14 to 16 hours a day!

People hunted beaver for their fur.

TYPES OF WATER

People canoe on many types of water. Calm ponds and lakes are great for beginners. They are also good for fishing. Some people like exploring

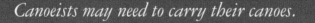

Canoeists may need to carry their canoes.

narrow streams. They have to get past **obstacles** such as fallen trees and shallow water. Others paddle for miles on broad rivers.

Adventurous people enjoy canoeing in **white water**. They **maneuver** through rushing water and around big rocks. Experts might even paddle down small waterfalls!

Often, people must travel between bodies of water. They take their canoes out of the water and carry them. This is called **portaging**. People also portage their canoes to get around rapids or water that is too shallow.

GETTING TO WATER

If someone rents a canoe, it is usually already near the water. But people who own canoes need to bring them to the water. Most people buy canoe racks for the tops of their cars. They need to know the right knots to tie the canoe down well.

Logs are common obstacles for canoeists.

CANOE COMPETITIONS

There are many different canoe races held around the world. In some events, canoeists brave a white water course. Quick turns test how well they maneuver. Other white water events are all about speed.

Canoe competitions can include white water.

Races on calmer water can be short and fast. Others are long events over 10 miles (16 km) or more. Some take several days and go hundreds of miles! In other races, people use a pole rather than a paddle. In some, sails are attached to the canoes.

Freestyle canoeing tests a person's control of the boat. Competitors perform to music. They show off with spins, turns, and fancy paddle work.

THE RIGHT EQUIPMENT

There are different canoe designs for every activity. The shape of the **hull** affects a canoe's speed and how easily it steers. It also affects how stable the canoe is in rough water.

Canoes for fishing are very stable. They might have a place to mount a small motor. Canoes for white water are light and easy to maneuver. Canoes for racing are fast in the

Many canoeists paddle all-purpose canoes.

water. Larger canoes hold more gear for long camping trips. All-purpose canoes work for many activities.

Canoe paddles have a single blade at the bottom. They have a handle to grip at the top. Paddles are made out of wood, light metal, or fiberglass. They come in special shapes for different activities. A person needs the right-sized paddle. If paddles are too small, they lose paddling power. If they are too large, they are hard to use.

Bringing a spare paddle is important. It is easy to lose or break a paddle!

CANOE CAMPING

Many people like to use canoes for camping trips. They pack all their gear in the canoe. They need a tent, sleeping bags, and cooking supplies. Then, they canoe to their campsites.

It's important to choose the right-sized paddle.

SAFETY GEAR

Everyone in a canoe needs a life jacket. A life jacket can only save your life if you are wearing it. It should not be stuck under a seat or used as a cushion.

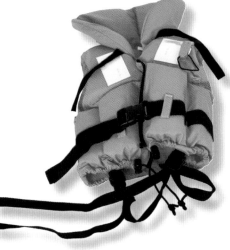

It is easy to get cold and wet on the water. People wear layers to keep warm. They choose fabrics that dry quickly. A hat and sunscreen are important, too. Sunglasses block the sun reflecting off the water.

Always wear a life jacket when you go canoeing.

Use a waterproof bag to store things
that cannot get wet. These include cameras,
binoculars, spare clothes, food, a **compass**,
and a first aid kit. Maps should be waterproof
or kept in plastic sleeves.

*A compass and map help canoeists
find their way.*

WATER SAFETY

Canoes float well. They are stable in calm water. But big waves or obstacles can make a canoe fill with water or tip. It is important to always wear a life jacket. The canoe should also carry a rope. It can be used to rescue people who have fallen out of the boat.

People can take canoe safety classes. They learn what to do if the canoe tips. They learn how to get water out of the canoe. They practice getting back into the canoe if they fall out.

Most tip-overs happen when people are getting into the canoe. Getting in a canoe can make it unstable. Crouch low to keep your balance. Step into the middle of

Canoeists should learn water safety, such as wearing a life jacket.

the canoe. This will help keep it from tipping.

Open boats such as canoes are exposed to the weather. It is important to check the forecast before going for a paddle. It is very dangerous to canoe in a thunderstorm. Lightning strikes can be deadly.

Even if it is not raining, people get wet in canoes. It can be colder and windier on the open water, too. A person can get sick from being wet and cold. Be prepared to get wet. Avoid becoming ill by dressing for the weather. Bring along an extra set of dry clothes.

Canoeing can be sweaty work. People often need to drink more water than they think they need while paddling. Not drinking enough water can cause dizziness or headaches.

Bring a water bottle when you go canoeing.

PADDLING THROUGH NATURE

Canoeing is a great way to experience nature. Canoeists can enjoy peaceful mornings on the water. Or they can get a thrill rushing

Paddle a canoe to experience nature a whole new way!

over rapids. They see birds, fish, or other wildlife. Paddling together teaches teamwork, too.

Spend the day in a canoe. Stop on a sandy shore and build a castle. Watch for turtles on logs. Splash the water with your paddle. Watch how rivers and lakes change with the seasons. Learn new things about nature. Canoeing can make memories that last your whole lifetime!

PROTECTING NATURE
Pollution can damage water habitats. Litter can kill fish, birds, and other animals. Be sure to pick up your trash. Do not pick flowers or take home rocks, either. Leave nature as you found it.

GLOSSARY

centuries (SEN-chur-eez): Centuries are periods of a hundred years. Native Americans have used canoes for centuries.

compass (KUM-puhs): A compass is a device that shows which way is north. People can use a map and a compass to find their way.

fiberglass (FYE-bur-glas): Fiberglass is a material made from tiny glass fibers and is very strong but lightweight. Some canoes are made of fiberglass.

hull (huhl): A hull is the body or frame of a boat. The hull of a canoe can be different shapes.

maneuver (mun-NOO-ver): To maneuver is to move something with care. People use their paddles to maneuver canoes.

obstacles (AHB-stuh-kuls): Obstacles are things that are in the way. Rocks and fallen trees can be obstacles for canoes.

paddle (PAD-uhl): To paddle is to use a type of short oar to steer and push along a boat. People paddle canoes to enjoy nature and have fun.

pollution (pu-LOO-shun): Pollution is waste and poison released into the environment. Pollution can be harmful to lakes, streams, and the plants and animals living in them.

portaging (POR-tij-ing): Portaging is carrying a canoe between two bodies of water. Portaging a canoe between lakes is common for canoeists.

rapids (RAP-idz): Rapids are fast-flowing parts of a river. Some people canoe over rapids.

transportation (trans-pur-TAY-shun): Transportation is a way of moving people or things from one place to another. Cars, bikes, and canoes are all means of transportation.

white water (WITE WAW-tur): White water is water moving quickly in a river that looks white as it passes over rocks. Some people like to canoe in white water.

wildlife (WYELD-lyef): Wildlife is the animals living in nature. You can see a lot of wildlife on a canoe trip.

TO LEARN MORE

BOOKS

Powell, Consie. *Leave Only Ripples: A Canoe Country Sketchbook*. Ely, MN: Raven Productions, 2005.

Slade, Suzanne. *Let's Go Canoeing and Kayaking*. New York: PowerKids Press, 2007.

Watson, Tom. *Kids Gone Paddlin': The Young Paddler's Guide to Having More Fun Outdoors*. Chanhassen, MN: Creative Publishing International, 2008.

WEB SITES

Visit our Web site for links about canoeing:
childsworld.com/links

Note to Parents, Teachers, and Librarians: We routinely verify our Web links to make sure they are safe and active sites. So encourage your readers to check them out!

INDEX